LIFE CYCLE OF BUTTERFLIES FOR KIDS

2nd Grade Science Edition Vol 4

BABY PROFESSOR

EDUCATION KIDS

Speedy Publishing LLC
40 E. Main St. #1156
Newark, DE 19711
www.speedypublishing.com

Butterflies have the
typical four-stage
insect life cycle.

A butterfly
starts life as
a very small,
round, oval or
cylindrical
egg.

Eggs are laid
on plants
by the adult
female
butterfly.

Butterfly eggs are protected by a hard-ridged outer layer of shell, called the chorion.

The egg stage lasts a few weeks in most butterflies.

The second stage is the caterpillar. A caterpillar is sometimes called larvae.

Caterpillars consume plant leaves and spend practically all of their time in searching for and eating food.

When a caterpillar is born, they are extremely small. When they start eating, they start growing and expanding.

As the
caterpillar
grows it splits
its skin and
sheds it about
4 or 5 times.

Stage three is
the chrysalis
also called
pupa. As
soon as a
caterpillar is
done growing
they form
themselves
into a
chrysalis.

Depending
on the
species, the
chrysalis may
suspended
under a
branch, hidden
in leaves
or buried
underground.

Within the chrysalis the old body parts of the caterpillar are undergoing a remarkable transformation, called metamorphosis.

This stage can last from a few weeks, a month or even longer.

Tissue, limbs
and organs of
a caterpillar
have all been
changed by
the time
the pupa is
finished.

Finally, when
the caterpillar
has done all
of its forming
and changing
inside the
pupa an adult
butterfly
emerges.

When the
butterfly first
comes out
its wings are
damp. The
wings are also
soft and are
folded against
its body.

The adults
have long legs,
long antennae,
and compound
eyes.

The adult's job is to mate and lay eggs.

Most adult butterflies live only one or two weeks, but some species hibernate during the winter and may live several months.

Visit

BABY PROFESSOR
EDUCATION KIDS

www.BabyProfessorBooks.com
to download Free Baby Professor eBooks
and view our catalog of new and exciting
Children's Books